GOD'S WORD
N STONE

HROUGH ARTISTS' EYES

N EXPLORATION OF BIBLE-INSPIRED ART | 6 STUDIES

Standard
PUBLISHING

Cincinnati, Ohio

Published by Standard Publishing, Cincinnati, Ohio
www.standardpub.com

Copyright © 2010 Standard Publishing

Written and developed by Joe Garland, Cindy Garland, and Jim Eichenberger

Cover design: Faceout Studio
Interior design: Dina Sorn at Ahaa! Design
Art Acquisition: Laura Derico

Photo Credits: **Sculptures by Michelangelo Buonarroti** (1475-1564): p. 4 *Moses*, 1513–16/ from the tomb of Pope Julius II, S. Pietro in Vincoli, Rome. Photo © Aprescindere | Dreamstime.com. p. 5 *Pieta*, 1499. Photo © Massimo Merlini | Dreamstime.com. *Rachel*, 1545 and *Leah*, 1545. Photo © Tanja Krstevska | Dreamstime.com. **Sculptures by Gian Lorenzo Bernini** (1598-1680): pp. 6, 7 *Habakkuk and the Angel* and *Daniel and the Lion*, 1655-1661. Marble. S. Maria del Popolo, Rome, Italy. Scala / Art Resource, NY. p. 7 *The Ecstasy of Teresa*, 1647-1652. S. Maria della Vittoria. Photo © adam eastland / Alamy. *David*, 1623-1624. Galleria Borghese, Rome, Italy. Scala / Art Resource, NY. **Sculptures by Giovanni Pisano** (1248-c. 1314): p. 8 Bust of *The Prophet Haggai*, from Siena Cathedral, Marble. Pisa, Italy, 1284-95. Copyright © V&A Images / All rights reserved. p. 9 *Miriam*, or *Maria di Mosè* and *Isaiah*, 1284-1296. Museo dell'Opera Metropolitana, Siena, Italy. Scala / Art Resource, NY. *Madonna with Child*, c. 1305-1306. Scrovegni Chapel, Padua, Italy. Alinari / Art Resource, NY. **Sculptures by Donatello** (c. 1386-1466): p. 10 *The Magdalen*, 1454-1455 and p. 11 *Prophet Jeremiah*, 1423-1427. Museo dell'Opera del Duomo, Florence, Italy. Scala / Art Resource, NY. p. 11 *Sacrifice of Isaac*, 1418. Museo dell'Opera del Duomo, Florence, Italy. Photo by Jastrow, Wikimedia Commons. *Saint Mark*, 1411-1413. Tabernacle of Linaioli, Rigattieri and Sarti, Church of Orsanmichele, Florence. Picture by Stefan Bauer, Wikimedia Commons, Creative Commons Attribution-Share Alike 2.5 Generic. **Sculptures by Alessandro Algardi** (1602-1654): p. 12 *The Beheading of St. Paul*, c. 1650. S. Paolo Maggiore, Bologna, Italy. Alinari / Art Resource, NY. p. 13 *Saint Matthew*, c. 1640. Ailsa Mellon Bruce Fund. Image courtesy National Gallery of Art, Washington. *Mary Magdalene* and *John the Evangelist*, 1628-1629. S. Silvestro al Quirinale, Rome. Photos © Alvaro de Alvariis, www.flickr.com/photos/dealvariis/. Used with permission. p. 14 *Christ in Majesty at Chartres*, mid 12th century. Royal Portal, West Façade, Chartres Cathedral, France. Photo © Piotr Golabek | Dreamstime.com. **Sculpture by Francois Duquesnoy** (1594-1643): p. 15 *Saint Andrew*, 1629-1633. St. Peter's Basilica, Vatican State. Wikimedia Commons. **Sculpture by Tilman Riemenschneider** (c. 1460-1531): p.15 *The Last Supper*, detail of the Holy Blood altar, c. 1501. St. Jacob's Church, Rothenburg ob der Tauber, Germany. Photo by Dr. Volkmar Rudolf. Creative Commons Attribution Share-Alike 3.0 Generic. **Sculpture by Luca della Robbia** (1399/1400-1482): p. 15 *Ascension*, 1446. Museo dell'Opera del Duomo, Florence, Italy. Scala / Art Resource, NY.

ISBN 978-0-7847-2488-0

16 15 14 13 12 11 10   1 2 3 4 5 6 7 8 9

CONTENTS

MOSES | 1513–1516

THE PIETA | 1499

RACHEL | 1545

LEAH | 1545

HABAKKUK AND THE ANGEL | 1655–1661

DANIEL AND THE LION | 1655–1661

THE ECSTASY OF TERESA | 1647–1652

DAVID | 1623–1624

THE PROPHET HAGGAI │ 1284–1295

MIRIAM, OR MARIA DI MOSÈ | 1284–1296

ISAIAH | 1284–1296

MADONNA WITH CHILD | c. 1305–1306

9

MARY MAGDALENE | 1454–1455

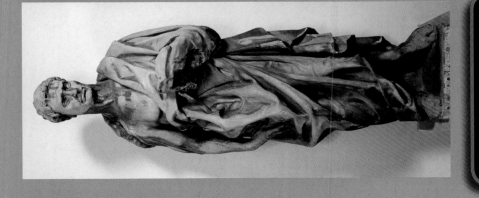

THE SACRIFICE
OF ISAAC | 1418

PROPHET JEREMIAH |
1423–1427

MARK | 1411–1413

11

BEHEADING OF PAUL │C. 1650

MATTHEW | c. 1640

MARY MAGDALENE | 1628–1629

JOHN THE EVANGELIST | 1628–1629

ANDREW | 1629–1633

THE LAST SUPPER | 1499–1505

THE ASCENSION OF CHRIST | 1446

HOW TO USE THESE STUDIES

God's Word in Stone is designed to help you learn more about great sculptures and the Book that inspired them. While we recommend that these studies be done in a group setting, they also can serve as engaging personal reading.

Each session follows this general outline:

SELECTING THE STONE | An introductory, group-building activity that allows you to share opinions about the big issue of the study.

ROUGHING OUT THE IMAGE | An examination of the work, life, and thoughts of the artist.

POLISHING THE ART | A Bible study that helps place the work of the artist within a biblical perspective.

DISPLAYING THE MASTERPIECE | Discussion that will help you apply the principles of the study to daily life.

In addition, the first page of each study contains a fun activity that can lead into initial discussion of the topic. If you have enough time in your session to begin this way, it can serve as a good group-building activity. It can also be "homework." Ask your members to look at that activity for the following session in preparation for the next meeting.

Finally, each session includes a page of resources. The Bible study resources can prepare the group leader to go even more deeply into the Scripture text of the session. A leader may want to have one or more of the art book resources available for the group to review. We also may suggest a video or other resource that could be used to augment a session at the leader's discretion.

The sculptures featured in this book have awed art lovers for years and years. Furthermore, the Book that was the inspiration for these masterpieces continues to touch the hearts of those who seek a deeper understanding of it. May you benefit in both ways from *God's Word in Stone!*

MOSES | MEETING GOD FACE TO FACE

SCULPTURE | Michelangelo's *Moses*

SCRIPTURE | Exodus 33:7-11; 34:29-35

THEME OF STUDY | God wants more than servants; he wants friends.

LOOK AT THE TEN means of communication listed below. Number them from 1 to 10—with 1 being the most impersonal means of communication (in your opinion) and 10 being the most personal.

_____ bulk e-mail
_____ cell phone call or text message
_____ group meeting
_____ landline phone call
_____ mailed form letter
_____ mailed personal letter
_____ one-on-one meeting
_____ personal e-mail
_____ posting on a social networking site (Facebook®, Twitter®, MySpace®)
_____ registered mail

List some of the messages you receive in the course of a month (for example: advertisements, family news, bills, information from your boss, etc.). For each type of message, think about the above and which means of delivery is appropriate and which is inappropriate.

Human beings are communicators! Sending and receiving messages is a part of our daily lives. But how does the nature of a relationship affect the way a message is sent and received?

SELECTING THE STONE

1 List the five people with whom you communicate the most in the course of a week.

2 *Why* do you communicate so much with these people? *How* do you choose to communicate with them? *What* types of things do you say to them?

3 Imagine that the president of the United States wanted to communicate to you. Why might he want to speak to you? What communication method might he choose? How would such communication change your life?

4 Imagine that God wanted to communicate to you. Answer the same questions listed above.

ROUGHING OUT THE IMAGE

Michelangelo Buonarroti was born in Caprese, Italy, on March 6, 1475. He died at almost 90 years of age on February 18, 1564. During most of his lifetime, Michelangelo was a celebrated artist of the Italian High Renaissance. During this time when there was an explosion of enthusiasm for scholarship and art, he was a painter, sculptor, poet, and architect.

1 Think of each of the four artistic disciplines Michelangelo practiced. What are some of the strengths of each of these means of communication? How might this versatility have contributed to his success as an artist?

Michelangelo believed the human body was the most important subject an artist could paint or sculpt. He studied anatomy by examining cadavers in a hospital in Florence. When sketching a design, Michelangelo often drew his subject naked first, then he would paint robes and other garments over his initial sketch, so he could make sure every muscle and curve were in their proper place.

2 Study the examples of Michelangelo's work on pages 4 and 5. Look for examples of detail given to the features of the bodies and the fit of their clothing. Agree or disagree with Michelangelo's idea that the human body was the most important subject of art.

The Pieta pictured on page 5 brought Michelangelo acclaim while he was still in his twenties, and it continues to be considered one of his greatest works. In fact, Michelangelo actually sculpted Mary holding the lifeless body of Jesus four times during his career. One pieta contained a self-portrait intended for his tomb. Another was his last work.

3 What might be the significance of Michelangelo returning time after time to the theme of the pieta?

In 1505, Michelangelo was asked to plan a huge tomb for Pope Julius II. Michelangelo created three statues for that tomb—*Moses, Rachel,* and *Leah.* Rachel and Leah were two wives of the patriarch Jacob (Genesis 29:16-30). Jacob married Rachel out of love, but was tricked into marrying Leah. Michelangelo used this account to contrast two ways people try to communicate with God—adoration and contemplation as opposed to work and religious activity.

4 Examine the images of *Rachel* and *Leah* on page 5. Notice physical features such as a tilt of the head, position of the hands, and muscular definition in arms and legs. Which woman represents the contemplative life and which the active life? How is this expressed?

The main sculpture considered in this session was completed after Michelangelo had finished his most notable painting—the ceiling of the Sistine Chapel. *Moses* took him four years to complete and portrays Moses after returning from Mount Sinai with the second set of stone tablets containing the Ten Commandments. The horns on Moses' head may be disconcerting to some who are accustomed to seeing the devil portrayed that way. The image actually comes from a mistranslation of Exodus 34:29-35 from Hebrew into Latin. The Hebrew word for *radiance* is similar to the word for *horn.*

5 Examine the image of this sculpture on page 4. Look at Moses' body language and facial expression and describe the mood of this work. Notice the direction Moses is looking and the position of the tablets. If this statue were to come to life, how would you feel about approaching Moses? Explain.

6 In his old age Michelangelo brooded increasingly about life after death. He was convinced that every day he lived made him less worthy of being in God's presence. What evidence of those fears do you see in this work completed decades earlier?

POLISHING THE ART

Moses has a unique place in biblical history. God chose Moses to be an intermediary between himself and the children of Israel. Read about that unique communication in Exodus 33:7-11.

1 Describe the details of the meetings between Moses and God. Try to explain the significance of the location of the tent in which the meeting took place. What might be the reason the pillar of cloud (indicating God's presence) stayed at the entrance of the tent when the meetings occurred?

2 How did the people of Israel who remained in the camp react to those meetings? How did Moses' protégé, Joshua, react after the meeting? Speculate on the motivations of each.

3 Other places in Scripture tell us that no one, including Moses, ever saw God's face. (See Exodus 33:20; John 1:18.) What, then, do you think is meant by Exodus 33:11a?

The Bible further describes some very strange details about the aftermath of Moses' meetings with God in Exodus 34:29-35.

4 Note that after God spoke to Moses, Moses made two separate presentations (vv. 31, 32). Why do you think that was done?

5 Describe how Moses used a veil (34:33-35). When did he put it on and take it off? How did the apostle Paul explain Moses' reason for using a veil when commenting on this event in 2 Corinthians 3:13?

Look again at Michelangelo's *Moses* on page 4. Note how Moses' appearance is frightening and that Moses' imposing form actually separates the people from the commandments of God. Paul describes how this separation between a holy God and sinful people was changed by Jesus in 2 Corinthians 3:3-18.

6 Look at 2 Corinthians 3:3. God communicated directly to Moses, but those words were passed on to the people through their leaders on stone tablets. How is God's communication with Christians more direct and personal?

7 Think of a time when you tried to change your behavior but failed. How does that explain how the law that Moses gave "condemns men" (2 Corinthians 3:9)? How does James 1:23, 24 explain how the glory of the law does not last within us but fades away?

8 Read 2 Corinthians 3:18, underlining the phrases "unveiled faces" and "ever-increasing glory." How does the gradual transformation that occurs because of the Holy Spirit living within us allow us to do what is described in James 1:25 and Romans 12:2?

DISPLAYING THE MASTERPIECE

Review these truths about a relationship with God found in the Bible texts we studied:

God's holiness makes communication with him desirable, but at the same time frightening. (See Exodus 33:7-11; 34:30.)

Knowing God only as a lawgiver results in "fading" relationships and distance from him. (See 2 Corinthians 3:13; James 1:23, 24.)

Through Jesus, God's Spirit can live within, slowly transforming and deepening our relationship with him. (See 2 Corinthians 3:3, 18; Romans 12:2.)

1 As mentioned earlier, Michelangelo spent the last years of his life convinced that every day he lived made him less worthy of being in God's presence. If you could talk to him during that stage of his life, what would you tell him based on the Scriptures above?

2 Each of the sculptures pictured on pages 4 and 5 illustrate a different type of relationship with God. Consider each one and decide how you are similar to or different from:

- Michelangelo's *Moses*—radiating God's holiness and anger at sin.

- Michelangelo's *Leah*—working hard to do right yet still feeling inadequate and unloved.

- Michelangelo's *Rachel*—convinced of God's love and feeling a mystical union with him.

- Mary in Michelangelo's *Pieta*—emotionally touched by realizing the pain Jesus experienced.

RESOURCES

BIBLE STUDY BOOKS

Swindoll, Charles. *Moses: A Man of Selfless Dedication.* Great Lives Series: Volume 4. (Thomas Nelson, 1999).

VIDEO

This skit portraying a fanciful discussion about how God wants to shape us could be used with any study in this book: http://www.skitguys.com/store/detail/188/

ART BOOKS

Langley, Andrew. *Michelangelo* (Raintree, 2003).

Neret, Gilles. *Michelangelo* (Taschen, 2006).

Tames, Richard. *The Life and Work of Michelangelo Buonarroti* (Reed Educational & Professional Publishing, Heinemann Library, 2001).

Venezia, Mike. *Michelangelo.* Getting to Know the World's Greatest Artists. (Children's Press, 1991).

POPULAR CULTURE

The story of Michelangelo (played by Charlton Heston) painting the Sistine Chapel was told in the classic film, *The Agony and the Ecstasy* (1965).

And of course, not only did Charlton Heston portray Michelangelo, but nine years earlier depicted Moses in *The Ten Commandments* (1956).

WEB SITES

http://www.abcgallery.com/M/michelangelo/michelangelo.html

http://www.biblegateway.com

HABAKKUK | TRUSTING GOD WHEN HE DOESN'T MAKE SENSE

SCULPTURE | Bernini's *Habakkuk and the Angel*

SCRIPTURE | Habakkuk 1:2-4; 3:16-19

THEME OF STUDY | Faith is tried when God does the unexpected.

TRY TO FINISH THIS top ten list.

You know you are having a bad day when . . .

10. you spill your entire cup of coffee in the lap of a gang member sitting next to you on the train.

9. your spouse calls you by the wrong name.

8. the candles on your birthday cake set off the fire alarm.

7. you see a wanted poster of your best friend in the post office.

6. paramedics come for a diner who just finished eating the same thing you are having.

5. you have a voice mail from an IRS agent.

4. your twin brother forgets your birthday.

3. _____

2. _____

And the number one reason you know you are having a bad day is . . .

1. _____

We all have a bad day now and then. But what if it's a *really* bad day? And what if your bad day lasts for weeks or months or years!

SELECTING THE STONE

1 Tell about one or two bad days you have had recently.

2 How did you handle your difficulties? How did your bad day affect your attitude toward yourself and others?

3 Think of a time when you or someone you know blamed God for hard times being experienced. Are we ever justified for blaming God for our problems? Why or why not?

4 Imagine that you were having the worst day of your life. Then imagine that God told you that he *allowed you* to experience the problems you were facing. What would you say to God?

ROUGHING OUT THE IMAGE

Gian Lorenzo Bernini was born in Naples, Italy, on December 7, 1598. Before the age of 20, Bernini was acclaimed a virtuoso sculptor, establishing his fame as the "Michelangelo of his age."

1 Think of some people who achieved "overnight" success. What are some results of achieving fame and fortune quickly?

At the age of 25, Bernini became the principal artist for the court of Pope Urban VIII. Bernini's passion for his Catholic faith and for using his art to explain it brought him international fame. But that fame did not last. Protestants in Europe considered Baroque art to be vulgar, lessening Bernini's influence there. When Innocent X ascended to the papacy, the new pope preferred other sculptors and architects. Although Bernini's popularity would rise to some extent later in his life, it was not until the mid-twentieth century that Bernini was again acclaimed as a virtuoso.

2 Bernini was motivated by his faith and certainly credited God for his success. How might he have felt about his fall from fame?

Later in his life Bernini experienced another setback. His right arm became paralyzed, hindering his expression of what he considered to be a God-given gift.

3 Do you think Christians are any better at handling problems than are unbelievers? Defend your opinion.

Bernini's father was a sculptor and trained his son in his workshop. Pietro Bernini would be described as a *mannerist*, a style of art that became popular in the closing years of the Renaissance. Mannerism tended to sculpt elegant characters that often appeared to be emotionally distant from the viewer.

Gian broke with his father's artistic tradition. The early seventeenth century saw a rise in popularity of the Baroque style, and the younger Bernini adopted that approach. Instead of self-conscious, almost icy characters, baroque artists showed flawed human beings dramatically engaged in life.

4 Briefly look at four Bernini sculptures pictured on pages 6 and 7. Point out how they illustrate these characteristics of baroque art.

5 Look at the sculpture of *David*. Great Renaissance artists such as Donatello, Verrocchio, and of course, Michelangelo depicted the account of David fighting the giant Goliath. From what you remember, how does this sculpture differ from those? Why might Bernini have dared to reimagine the work of such great artists?

While the other artists portrayed David's victorious pose after defeating Goliath (Verrocchio even includes the giant's decapitated head in his work!), Bernini pictures the outcome as of yet uncertain. David's body is twisted uncomfortably as he prepares to shoot a single stone at Goliath.

This idea of God working despite human hardship is also found in the other images on pages 6 and 7.

- *Daniel and the Lion* pictures the prophet being unjustly punished. In Daniel 6 the Bible explains that the prophet was sentenced to death because he dared to pray to God rather than the king.

- *The Ecstasy of Teresa* pictures a vision of Catholic mystic Teresa of Ávila. She tells of an angel appearing to her and piercing her heart with a flaming spear. She explained the vision as how the love of God can bring joy from pain.

- *Habakkuk and the Angel* is the main selection of this study. The account pictured comes from an apocryphal story, *Bel and the Dragon*. In this story, an angel drags the prophet Habakkuk by the hair to get him to deliver food to Daniel in the lion's den.

6 Examine all four sculptures and describe what Bernini was saying about the pain associated with following God.

POLISHING THE ART

The story pictured in *Habakkuk and the Angel* comes from a book that is accepted by the Catholic Church but not by Judaism or most Protestant churches. Because *Bel and the Dragon* and other books were rejected by the Reformation but affirmed by the Catholic Church in the Counter-Reformation, Bernini used images from it to affirm the Catholic Church's view.

Nevertheless, Catholics, Jews, and Protestants all accept the writings of the prophet Habakkuk found in the book in the Bible that bears his name. Habakkuk wrote about having faith in God during times of distress.

1 At the time of Habakkuk, the nation of Babylon (modern-day Iraq) was a rising power and was threatening to invade Judah. Read Habakkuk 1:2-4 and try to summarize the prophet's complaint.

2 What surprises you about the tone Habakkuk uses to address God?

3 Compare and contrast this complaint to Abraham's reaction to God upon learning that he planned to destroy Sodom and Gomorrah (Genesis 18:16-33).

4 Read God's response to Habakkuk in Habakkuk 1:5-11. How is this response different from what you might expect? Refer to Romans 8:18-28 and Hebrews 12:7-13 and try to explain what God was doing.

5 God's first response did not satisfy the prophet. Try to paraphrase Habakkuk's question in Habakkuk 1:13. From your view of evil in the world, do you think it is a good question?

6 Paraphrase God's response from Habakkuk 2:3, 20. When have you been given a similar response when you questioned the existence of evil and suffering? How satisfying was it for you? Explain.

7 Underline the one word common in all of these commands given to the people of Israel centuries before Habakkuk: Deuteronomy 8:2, 18; 15:15; 16:12; 24:9, 18, 22; 32:7. Why do you think that command is so important that it is repeated many times?

8 We see a turning point in Habakkuk's thinking in Habakkuk 3:2. How does that statement show that his thinking changed when he remembered how God had worked in the past?

9 Habakkuk's dark and depressing prophecy ends in a surprisingly upbeat song. Analyze Habakkuk 3:16-19 by trying to paraphrase:

verse 16: How Habakkuk felt—

verse 17: What Habakkuk did not have—

verse 18: The promise Habakkuk made—

verse 19: Habakkuk's statement of belief—

DISPLAYING THE MASTERPIECE

Review what the prophet Habakkuk said about God and human suffering:

It is natural for us to be bewildered and even angry when we face suffering. (See Habakkuk 1:2-4.)

Because God is all-powerful and loving, he is capable of taking even the worst situation and using it to shape us into what he wants us to be. (See Habakkuk 2:20; Romans 8:28; Hebrews 12:10, 11.)

Even in the midst of suffering we can live with the assurance that God is working and will give us the strength to endure. (See Habakkuk 3:16-19.)

1 Think back to a point in your life when you faced a problem that you thought of as almost insurmountable at the time. Was that problem ever resolved? If so, how?

2 Think about a current issue in your life that makes you question (even for a moment) what God has in store for you. Which of the following approaches might be appropriate for you to take at this point?

- Tell God about your confusion and even your anger in prayer.

- Examine your life and see how facing a challenge may be making you a better person.

- Remember other times when life was rough but God was faithful.

RESOURCES

BIBLE STUDY BOOKS

Bruckner, James. *Jonah, Nahum, Habakkuk, Zephaniah.* The NIV Application Commentary. (Zondervan, 2004).

Robertson, O. Palmer. *The Books of Nahum, Habakkuk, and Zephaniah.* The New International Commentary on the Old Testament. (Eerdmans, 1990).

ART BOOKS

Kessel, Dmitri and Henri Peyre. *Splendors of Christendom: Great Art and Architecture in European Churches* (Edita Lausanne, 1964).

Manca, Joseph, Patrick Bade, and Sarah Costello. *1000 Sculptures of Genius* (Sirrocco, 2007).

Toman, Rolf, ed. *Baroque: Architecture, Sculpture, Painting* (Tandem Verlag, 2007).

POPULAR CULTURE

In his novel *Angels and Demons* and the 2009 film based on it, Dan Brown features two of the Bernini sculptures from this session. Brown's work has absolutely no basis in fact, but has led to a resurgence of interest in Bernini in popular culture.

WEB SITES

This site is in Italian, but features images of much of Bernini's work: http://www.scultura-italiana.com/Biografie/Bernini.htm

http://www.biblegateway.com

HAGGAI | PROCLAIMING GOD WHEN PEOPLE ARE TOO BUSY TO LISTEN

SCULPTURE | Giovanni Pisano's *Haggai*

SCRIPTURE | Haggai 1:1-15

THEME OF STUDY | Proclaiming God to the prosperous is a grueling task.

NEWS FLASH!

Try to match the news headline with the date it occurred. (The older you are, the easier this may be!)

_____ 1. Hawaii Becomes 50th State
_____ 2. Paris Liberated by Allied Forces
_____ 3. Pope John Paul II Shot in Vatican Square
_____ 4. East Meets West: Transcontinental Railroad Completed
_____ 5. High Court Rules Abortions Legal
_____ 6. Emancipation Proclamation Frees Southern Slaves
_____ 7. Capone Convicted of Tax Evasion
_____ 8. King Tut's Tomb Opened
_____ 9. Hijacked Jets Destroy Twin Towers
_____ 10. Gandhi Is Killed; India Shaken

a. September 22, 1862
b. May 10, 1869
c. February 16, 1923
d. October 19, 1931
e. August 25, 1944
f. January 30, 1948
g. Aug. 21, 1959
h. January 22, 1973
i. May 13, 1981
j. September 11, 2001

Which of these events do you think is of the most consequence? Which is of the least importance to you?

Answers: 1. g, 2. e, 3. i, 4. b, 5. h, 6. a, 7. d, 8. c, 9. j, 10. f

Occasionally, news of such importance will occur that it will disrupt the daily routines of life. What are some of the most significant historical events of your lifetime?

SELECTING THE STONE

1 Below is a list of sources from which important information may come. For each source describe a message that you would consider life-changing:

- a news bulletin interrupting a popular TV program.

- a midnight phone call from a parent.

- a registered letter from an attorney.

- a phone call from your physician.

2 Select one or two of your responses from above. For each one tell about:

- something you complained about before the announcement that now seems trivial.

- something you had put off doing before the announcement that has now become a high priority.

- a relationship that had not been nurtured before the announcement that has now become very important.

ROUGHING OUT THE IMAGE

Giovanni Pisano was born into an Italian family of sculptors and architects in 1250. His father, Nicola Pisano, was the earliest noted Italian sculptor and the last working in the medieval classical style. Working with his father early in his career, Giovanni was a prolific sculptor. Their last work before Nicola's death was *Fontana Maggiore,* a large fountain in the public square of Perugia in 1278. Father and son designed twenty-four statues and forty-eight reliefs for that project, all finished within that year!

1 Tell about a time when you were extremely productive. What motivated you to work especially hard during that time? Does that motivation still drive you to be productive? Explain.

While his father was a classicist, Giovanni took that medieval artistic style and blended it with the Gothic style emerging in France. The result was a highly expressive, emotionally charged and dramatic style rich in contrasts. Pisano was also the first sculptor in Tuscany to incorporate statues into the architecture.

2 Why do you think it is difficult to break with tradition? What conflicts might Pisano have faced by breaking with the family style and with the accepted artistic norms of the day?

For most of the last two decades of the thirteenth century, Pisano worked as the architect for a new cathedral in Siena. The fourteen life-size sculptures he carved for the facade of the cathedral comprised some of the outstanding work of his career. Most figures were of biblical prophets, but also included influential Greek thinkers such as Plato and Aristotle.

3 How do you react to the fact that Pisano included nonbiblical characters in the façade of a cathedral? If you were to add two modern persons to his work, who would they be and why?

Turn to pages 8 and 9 and examine the following sculptures from the Siena Cathedral found there:

Maria di Mosè (Miriam, the sister of Moses)—Miriam is described as a prophetess in the Bible. Miriam was with the Israelites when they crossed the Red Sea and led the people in a song of celebration.

Isaiah—After the reigns of King David and King Solomon, God's people began to stray from him. During that time the prophet Isaiah warned that this would bring consequences, but also pointed to a coming king (the Christ) who would rule forever in a perfect kingdom.

Haggai—After God punished Israel and Judah, allowing their homeland to be destroyed and the people to be sent into exile, the Jews were allowed to return home. The prophet Haggai warned those who returned to place God, not themselves, first.

4 Describe the expressions on the sculptures' faces, the position of their bodies, and any other details you find interesting. What do those things communicate to you?

Pisano sculpted these prophets to display emotion, activity, and anticipation. Note that all three of these characters have their heads turned away from the directions their bodies are facing, indicating something or someone demanded their attention. In the façade of the cathedral in Siena, these figures are all turned to face a sculpture of Mary, Jesus' mother.

Just as the Pieta was a favorite subject of Michelangelo (see Session 1), Pisano sculpted the image of Mary holding the infant Jesus a number of times. One of those sculptures of the Madonna with child is on page 9.

5 Why do you think this was a favorite subject of Pisano? What was he saying by having biblical and nonbiblical wise men and women turning their gaze in her direction in his work on the Siena Cathedral?

POLISHING THE ART

Pisano's sculpture of the prophet Haggai is found on page 8. Note the sense of urgency and warning that Pisano tried to express in the facial features and body language of this figure.

Haggai prophesied to the people of Israel after they had returned to their homeland. They had been taken captive seven decades earlier and had lived in exile. Many Israelites returned with a leader named Zerubbabel for the purpose of rebuilding their war-ravaged land.

1 Read Haggai 1:1-4. What seems to be the occasion for this book?

2 Take the side of the people of Israel for a moment. How might they have answered Haggai's question from verse 4? Why might that answer be a logical response for people returning to their family land after it had lain in ruins for seven decades?

3 Read Haggai's words in verse 6. Prophets sometimes used very pointed, satirical humor to make their points. Explain the humor in the prophet's ironic statement.

4 Compare verse 6 with the words of another Old Testament prophet in Jeremiah 2:13. How are the images they use similar? How were the people of Haggai's day guilty of the same two sins Jeremiah described?

The book of James in the New Testament was written to people who were very familiar with the words of the Old Testament prophets. James addressed a problem in the church in which wealthy believers felt superior to poorer believers.

5 Paraphrase James 1:9-11. Explain his use of irony in these verses. How is this message similar to those of Haggai and Jeremiah?

6 Turn to James 4:13-16. Underline the question James asks in verse 14. How might most people (including the people in Haggai's day) answer it? How does James's answer make you feel? Explain.

7 Read Haggai 1:12-15. How did the people respond to the message of the prophet? While we think of fear as something negative, when can fear be a good thing?

8 Circle the four-word response of God in verse 13. Refer to the following verses to explain the importance of that answer:

• Deuteronomy 31:6-8

• Psalm 118:7-9

• Matthew 6:31-33

DISPLAYING THE MASTERPIECE

Review the counsel of the prophet Haggai we just examined.

When we are busy, we tend to place caring for our physical needs before our need to worship (Haggai 1:1-4).

Our attempts to construct a perfect life of our own making will inevitably fail at some point (Haggai 1:5-11; Jeremiah 2:13; James 4:13-17).

Making the search for God's will and presence in our lives a priority will allow both material and spiritual needs to be fulfilled (Haggai 1:12-15; Matthew 6:31-33).

1 With those ideas in mind, try to formulate a biblical response to each of the following statements someone might make:

- "I will go to church after I get my career off to a solid start."

- "I don't get it! I work and scrimp and save and never seem to get ahead."

- "Religion is just a way for the poor and weak to feel better about their situation."

2 Which of the above thoughts have you had most recently? What do you need to do in order to take your own advice?

RESOURCES

BIBLE STUDY BOOKS

Baldwin, Joyce G. *Haggai, Zechariah, Malachi.* Tyndale Old Testament Commentaries. (Tyndale, 2009).

Boda, Mark J. *Haggai, Zechariah.* The NIV Application Commentary. (Zondervan, 2004).

Verhoef, Pieter A. *The Books of Haggai and Malachi.* The New International Commentary on the Old Testament. (Eerdmans, 1987).

ART BOOKS

Chilvers, Ian, ed. *The Concise Oxford Dictionary of Art & Artists* (Oxford University Press, 2005).

Duby, Georges and Jean-Luc Daval, eds. *Sculpture from Antiquity to the Middle Ages* (Taschen, 2006).

Janson, H. W. *History of Art* (Prentice-Hall, 1973).

Williamson, Paul. *Gothic Sculpture, 1140–1300* (Yale University Press, 1995).

WEB SITES

http://www.nndb.com/people/894/000084642/

http://www.biography.com/articles/Giovanni-Pisano-9441672

http://www.answers.com/topic/giovanni-pisano

http://www.biblegateway.com

MARY MAGDALENE | LOVING GOD WHEN OTHERS SAY YOU DON'T DESERVE HIM

SCULPTURE | Donatello's *Mary Magdalene*

SCRIPTURE | Luke 8:1-3

THEME OF STUDY | God can salvage lives that have been savaged.

CREATE AN ACROSTIC BY using a word or phrase describing yourself that begins with each of the six letters below.

M _____

Y _____

S _____

E _____

L _____

F _____

How well would someone know you just from this information? What else would you like to add?

How well do others know "the real you"? Is that a bad thing? a good thing? maybe a little of both?

SELECTING THE STONE

1 Tell about a time . . .

when you felt great about yourself.

when you felt terrible about yourself.

when you realized someone was not the person you thought he or she was.

2 Complete the following sentences:

When I see someone wearing _____ ,

I immediately think they are _____ .

When I hear someone _____ ,

I immediately think _____ .

3 Our observations are important, but may not always tell the whole story. How can you be realistic without becoming cynical?

ROUGHING OUT THE IMAGE

Donatello was born Donato di Niccolo di Betto Bardi in Florence, Italy, in 1386. During the course of his 80-year life span, he proved himself to be a master sculptor of marble, bronze, clay, and wood. He is known as the most important and influential sculptor of the Italian Early Renaissance and as one of the greatest of all Italian Renaissance artists. At the time of his death, Donatello had created countless works that would guide entire generations of later sculptors.

1 What do you think contributes to someone having lasting influence in a particular field? Before looking into the work of Donatello more deeply, list some qualities you might expect to find in an artist who was considered to be an influence for generations to come.

One of the innovations of Donatello was his bringing an increased realism, emotional intensity, and psychological insight to his art. He not only achieved a technical excellence rivaling that of the ancient masters of sculpture, but he also went beyond them in endowing his figures with a sense of humanity. Most of his work has the power that comes only from stark simplicity and unblinking realism.

2 Think of the most realistic work of classical or popular art (anything from a classic painting to a popular movie) you have ever experienced. What is the value of realism in a work of art?

3 Is it possible for art to be too realistic? What subjects would you prefer *not* to be portrayed realistically? Explain.

These three marble sculptures by Donatello are pictured on page 11:

The Sacrifice of Isaac—After waiting decades for a son, God called upon Abraham to prove his faith by being willing to sacrifice that son (Genesis 22:1-19).

Prophet Jeremiah—Jeremiah was sometimes called the "weeping prophet" because God assigned him to deliver the painful message that his nation would be conquered and taken captive (Jeremiah 1:14-16; 9:1).

Mark—Mark, the writer of the second Gospel, was characterized as impulsive and even unreliable in his youth (Mark 14:51, 52; Acts 15:37, 38). Yet in his later years he was respected among the apostles (2 Timothy 4:11).

4 Examine the photos of these three sculptures. Point out evidences of realism in their proportions, anatomical features and posture, facial expressions, and correspondence to the historical characters and situations they display.

Unlike the preceding featured sculptures in these studies, the work pictured on page 10 was carved from wood. *Mary Magdalene* portrays Mary from the town of Magdala, a woman briefly mentioned in all four Gospels, but about whom speculation has been rife for centuries. Fanciful stories written long after the Gospels describe her as everything from a leader of an early Christian sect to a prostitute to the wife of Jesus. All of these extra-biblical theories have been advanced with very specific agendas and with little or no evidence, so their credibility is suspect.

5 Describe Dontatello's depiction of Mary Magdalene, paying close attention to details such as facial features, position of her arms and hands, dress (or lack thereof), and general physical condition. List some single words you would use to describe the sculpture.

6 In his latter years, when he carved this sculpture, Donatello was in poor health. How might that have affected his choice of subject, his portrayal of her, and even the medium he used?

POLISHING THE ART

All four Gospels record that Mary Magdalene was a witness of the resurrection of Jesus. But Luke 8:1-3 gives some additional information.

1 Notice Mary's affliction before being a follower of Jesus. Describe the condition of others with the same affliction in the following passages and speculate how Mary might have lived before meeting Jesus:

- Mark 5:1-5

- Mark 9:17-20

- Acts 16:16-19

Common wisdom often teaches that genetics and past training irrevocably shape a person. The biblical view, however, is that God can and does radically transform those who come to him.

2 Read Paul's words in 2 Corinthians 5:16, 17. Paraphrase it so that it talks specifically about Mary Magdalene.

3 Luke 8:1-3 describes a tremendous lifestyle change for Mary. Refer to her story and the following verses to speculate on how her life changed in regard to:

• her companions (2 Corinthians 6:14-18).

• her view of material goods (Ephesians 4:28).

• her hope for the future (2 Corinthians 4:16-18).

Mary's final appearance in the Gospels is found in John 20:10-18. Note that at first she desired only to locate Jesus' lifeless body, fully believing that he was dead (v. 15). When she realized Jesus was alive, she ran to him. Many translations render Jesus' command to her as "Do not cling to me" (v. 17).

4 Knowing the change Jesus had made in her life, explain why Mary, more than any of the others, desired to locate Jesus' body and then to hold him so tightly that he had to command her to release him.

5 Describe the new mission Jesus had for Mary and how she went about fulfilling it (vv. 17, 18).

DISPLAYING THE MASTERPIECE

Review the brief outline of the life of Mary Magdalene based on the texts we have just examined.

While we have no details of the life of Mary prior to her following Jesus, it is likely that demon possession resulted in physical decay, social exile, and subjugation to the most unscrupulous people in her society (Luke 8:2; Mark 5:1-5; Mark 9:17-20; Acts 16:16-19).

In following Jesus, Mary found like-minded companions, used her material goods for the furtherance of the gospel, and looked forward to the coming kingdom of God (Luke 8:1-3).

Although Mary mourned her physical separation from Jesus, she gladly accepted his call to tell others about his resurrection (John 20:10-18).

1 Look again at Donatello's wooden sculpture on page 10. This time, knowing what happened to Mary, tell why it is beautiful despite being ugly.

2 Which of the following actions would be most appropriate for you to take as a result of this session?

- Renounce a part of your life that has done damage to you physically, emotionally, or socially.

- Begin to regard an outcast you know as someone whom God loves and can transform.

- Look for a specific action you can take to further the spread of the gospel.

RESOURCES

BIBLE STUDY BOOKS

Higgs, Liz Curtis. *Unveiling Mary Magdalene* (WaterBrook Press, 2004).

McDowell, Josh. *The DaVinci Code: A Quest for Answers* (Green Key Books, 2006).

ART BOOKS

Toman, Rolf. *The Art of the Italian Renaissance: Architecture, Sculpture, Painting, Drawing* (Tandem Verlag, 2005).

Wirtz, Rolf C. *Donatello.* Masters of Italian Art Series. (Konemann, 1998).

POPULAR CULTURE

Mary Magdalene has inspired many popular songs over the years. They include:

"If Jesus Ever Loved a Woman" by Johnny Cash

"Lights of Magdala" by Johnny Cash

"Mary Magdalene" by Patty Larkin

"I Don't Know How to Love Him" from *Jesus Christ Superstar* by Andrew Lloyd Webber and Tim Rice

WEB SITES

http://www.wga.hu/bio/d/donatell/biograph.html

http://www.scultura-italiana.com/biografie/donatello.htm

http://www.biblegateway.com

PAUL | SERVING GOD TO THE VERY END

SCULPTURE | Algardi's *Beheading of Paul*

SCRIPTURE | 2 Timothy 4:6-8

THEME OF STUDY | Success in life is measured by the way we finish it.

WENDY NORTHCUTT HAS PRESENTED The Darwin Awards since 1985 to people who have had fatal accidents because of their own stupidity. Here are a few examples:

April 1999

A German sword swallower exhibited his skill by sliding an umbrella down his throat. He died of suffocation after he accidentally pushed the button that opened it.

May 2001

A Croatian college student demonstrated his juggling ability to fellow students. His choice of objects to juggle—live hand grenades—killed him and injured six spectators.

March 2005

A Vietnamese man found an old detonator while he and his friends were drinking at a construction site. He bet the others that it was too old to explode. To prove his point, the man placed the detonator in his mouth and had his friends plug the wires dangling from it into an electrical outlet. The man lost his wager and his life.

July 2009

A South Carolina man robbed an electronics store at gunpoint. He believed he could conceal his identity by spray painting his face black before the robbery. Not only was the disguise ineffectual, it was deadly. Inhalation of the toxic chemicals foiled the thief even before police caught up with him.

Darwin argued that a species would improve because the unfit would die off, leaving the superior beings to continue the biological line. But is competition *really* the path to perfection?

SELECTING THE STONE

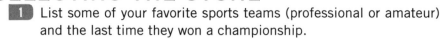 List some of your favorite sports teams (professional or amateur) and the last time they won a championship.

2 Are you only loyal to those teams if they win championships? If not, list a few other reasons for your loyalty.

3 Finish these sayings about winning and losing, and add any others you can think of. Tell whether you agree or disagree with each one and why.

- It's not whether you win or lose . . .

- Winning isn't everything, it's the . . .

- Winners never quit, and quitters . . .

ROUGHING OUT THE IMAGE

Born at the end of the sixteenth century in Bologna, Italy, Alessandro Algardi studied art at the Carracci Academy in his hometown. Bologna had no native stone, so in his early career Algardi sculpted in terracotta (clay) and stucco (plaster).

> **1** Tell about a time you had to improvise and make do with what you had. What were the results? What effect did that have in the development of your skills?

Algardi became known for his terracotta bust portraitures. The dignity and detail of these busts made him one of the most sought-after portraitists of his day. Algardi was also known for his restoration of classical Greek and Roman sculpture, and the influence of classicism was obvious in his work.

> **2** An example of his terracotta portraits is *Matthew*, pictured on page 13. Point out some of the features in this bust discussed in the preceding paragraph.

Algardi's earliest important works were a pair of over life-size stucco statues of John the Evangelist and Mary Magdalene (1628–1629) for wall niches of the chapel of Cardinal Ottavio Bandini in San Silvestro al Quirinale. These are also pictured on page 13.

> **3** Compare and contrast Algardi's sculpture of Mary Magdalene to Donatello's impression of the same biblical character created two centuries earlier (p. 10). What might be some reasons Algardi's take was so different from Donatello's? (Consider the reason for the work, the influences of both artists, and the stage Algardi was in his career.)

Bernini (Session 2 in this book) was a contemporary of Algardi and his chief rival. Bernini employed the emotive Baroque style, while Algardi was greatly influenced by the sobriety and realism of classical sculpture.

4 Compare and contrast Algardi's sculptures on page 13 to Bernini's work pictured on pages 6 and 7. You may also wish to review the discussion of Bernini on pages 27 and 28. Explain why you believe the two artists were rivals in their day.

During the papacy of Innocent X (1644–1655), Bernini fell out of favor with the pope, and Algardi replaced Bernini as the principal artist for the church. It was during this papacy that Algardi came to true artistic prominence.

5 From what you remember from Session 2, how lasting was this victory over Bernini? What are some examples today of trends and styles changing back and forth over the years?

Algardi's masterpiece, *Beheading of Paul*, was commissioned in 1634 by Virgilio Spada, a patron well established in Bologna. This dramatic altarpiece for the church of San Paolo Maggiore illustrates the traditional belief that Paul was executed by the Romans during Nero's reign.

6 Examine the picture of this work on page 12. How does this compare and contrast with other works of Algardi we have viewed? Looking at the facial expression of Paul, how does it compare to what you might expect of one about to lose his life in a matter of seconds? Explain whether you think Algardi is portraying Paul as a winner or a loser.

POLISHING THE ART

Paul (Saul) of Tarsus was trained as a rabbi; because of his zeal, he persecuted the early church (Galatians 1:13). After his conversion to Christianity, however, he became a missionary and founded churches throughout Asia Minor and Greece (Acts 13–19). He was arrested and sent to Rome to stand trial for treason, a charge often made because of his belief that Jesus was the promised Messiah. (See Acts 17:7, for example.) Tradition tells us that he was cleared of that charge and released, only to be arrested later and executed.

1 Read 2 Timothy 4:6-8. Underline words or phrases that indicate that Paul knew his death was imminent.

2 Notice the word *offering* Paul used in verse 6. Refer to the following verses to help clarify what Paul meant by that word:

• Romans 12:1

• Matthew 16:24, 25

• 1 Peter 2:21-24

3 Describe the feeling you have after completing a difficult task. Notice the two images Paul used to describe his life to that point in 2 Timothy 4:7. Clarify his meaning by summarizing these verses as well:

• 1 Timothy 1:18-20

- 1 Corinthians 9:24-27

- Galatians 5:7

- Hebrews 12:1-3

4 List some things that motivate people to achieve. What awards or rewards motivate you?

5 Describe the reward (crown) that motivated the early Christians by paraphrasing these verses:

- Philippians 4:1

- 1 Thessalonians 2:17-19

- James 1:12-18

- 1 Peter 5:1-4

6 Look again at Algardi's depiction of Paul's execution. From what we have just discussed, imagine a cartoon thought balloon over Paul's head. List some possible thoughts going through his mind at that time.

DISPLAYING THE MASTERPIECE

Review the last words of apostle Paul based on the texts we have just examined.

Paul did not see his execution as defeat, but rather an offering to God in service to others that was modeled after the sacrificial offering Jesus made for the entire world (2 Timothy 4:6; 1 Peter 2:19-24).

Paul looked back on his life without regrets, believing that he had accomplished what he had been called to do (2 Timothy 4:7; Hebrews 12:1-3).

Paul expected the reward of being counted as righteous by God, having the eternal life promised by him, and being reunited with believers with whom he had shared the gospel (2 Timothy 4:8; James 1:12-18; 1 Thessalonians 2:17-19).

1 Review the list above. Which do you find easiest to accept? Which is hardest for you to accept? What can you do to become more convinced?

2 Do you know of anyone who believes Christians are candidates for Darwin Awards? That is, they believe that Christians squander their lives because of having beliefs they consider to be stupid? How would you answer such statements if given the opportunity?

RESOURCES

BIBLE STUDY BOOKS

Stott, R. W. *Message of 2 Timothy: Guard the Gospel* (InterVarsity Press, 1973).

Wiersbe, Warren W. *Be Faithful* (David C. Cook, 1981).

ART BOOKS

Chilvers, Ian, ed. *The Concise Oxford Dictionary of Art & Artists* (Oxford University Press, 2005).

Duby, Georges and Jean-Luc Daval, eds. *Sculpture: From the Renaissance to the Present Day* (Taschen, 2006).

Strickland, Carol. *The Illustrated Timeline of Art History* (Sterling Publishing, 2006).

WEB SITES

http://www.artcyclopedia.com/artists/algardi_alessandro.html

http://www.wga.hu/bio/a/algardi/biograph.html

http://www.answers.com/topic/alessandro_algardi

http://www.biblegateway.com

THE APOSTLES | AWAITING GOD AND THE FULFILLMENT OF HIS PROMISES

SCULPTURE | *The Apostles* in Chartres Cathedral

SCRIPTURE | Matthew 28:16-20; Acts 1:1-14

THEME OF STUDY | Followers of Jesus have work to do before the world draws to an end.

W AITING . . .

It seems there is always something "just around the corner" that we anticipate. Think for a moment and calculate (aren't you glad most cell phones have calculators!) the amount of time that will pass before each of these events:

- number of days until your favorite holiday.

- number of months until your next "milestone" birthday.

- number of minutes until the next time you eat.

- number of hours until the weekend.

- number of seconds until this exercise is over.

What else would you add to this list?

"I can hardly wait!" How often do we say or think that in our lives? But is life about waiting for the next big event, or is there something more significant that happens during life's intermissions?

SELECTING THE STONE

1 It has been said, "Life is what happens while you are busy making other plans."

- What does that mean to you?

- How have you seen it to be true in your own life?

2 How have you heard people complete the following thoughts?

- When I am financially on my feet, I will . . .

- When my schedule clears up a little, I will . . .

- When the kids are grown, I will . . .

- When I retire, I will . . .

In your experience, do people usually follow through on those kinds of promises? Explain.

ROUGHING OUT THE IMAGE

Jesus' twelve disciples have been of interest to Christians throughout the centuries. These twelve men followed and learned (*disciple* means "student") from Jesus over his three-year ministry. They were also sent out (*apostle* means "one sent on a mission") by Jesus to preach and to teach.

> **1** Tell some things you know about the twelve. How many can you name? (See Matthew 10:2-4.) Is it easier to recall facts about individual disciples or about the disciples as a group? What might be significant about that?

A portrayal of a nonbiblical account of Andrew, brother of Peter, is pictured on page 15. Francois Duquesnoy was a Flemish sculptor working in Rome about the same time as Bernini and Algardi. In his *Andrew,* Duquesnoy depicts Andrew's death. Tradition tells us that this disciple was crucified in Patras, Greece, on an X-shaped cross. (The X is the Greek letter *chi,* the first letter of the name Christ in Greek.)

> **2** Compare and contrast *Andrew* to the works of Bernini on pages 6 and 7 and of Algardi on pages 12 and 13. Note facial expressions, positions of the hands, and body posture. How do you think Andrew is dealing with his impending death in this portrayal?

About 130 years before Duquesnoy's *Andrew,* German sculptor Tilman Riemenschneider portrayed the biblical event of *The Last Supper* in the wood sculpture seen on page 15. Note that Jesus and an apostle holding a money bag (see John 12:4-6) draw the viewer's attention to the center of the carving.

3 Consider the expressions on the faces of the apostles, their body language, and the way their bodies are positioned. Choose a few of the apostles pictured, and try to guess what each one might be thinking at the time.

About half a century before Riemenschneider's *The Last Supper,* Italian sculptor Luca della Robbia portrayed another biblical event, *The Ascension of Christ* (Acts 1:9).

4 Contrast the portrayal of the apostles in this terracotta relief on page 15 with the chaos and division Riemenschneider pictured. Even though the Last Supper and Ascension occurred about a month and a half apart, what happened that might explain such a change in the entire mood of the events?

Three centuries before della Robbia, unnamed medieval artists had already begun to turn the Gothic cathedral at Chartres, France, into a virtual Bible story library of painting, stained glass, and sculpture. The carved facade over the central portal (grand doorway) of the cathedral is pictured on page 14. It shows the beginning of Christ's judgment of the world as described in Revelation 5:8-14, an event eagerly anticipated by Christians.

5 Think of the usual images that come to mind when one thinks of divine judgment. How does this work differ from those images? Describe some emotions one might experience when walking into the cathedral, passing under this facade.

Unlike classic Greek sculpture and the art of the Renaissance that would come later, this Gothic sculpture is much more symbolic than it is realistic. In the center is Jesus in a warm, welcoming pose surrounded by an egg-shaped frame called a *mandorla.* Symbolic representations of the four Gospel writers (Matthew as an angel,

Mark as a winged lion, Luke as a winged ox, and John as an eagle) surround Jesus. Below them are fourteen figures. The twelve apostles are grouped into four groups of three each, bounded by the prophet Elijah (1 Kings 17ff) on the left and Enoch (Genesis 5:24) on the right.

6 When we think of the way we use the number 3 (such as in the Trinity) and the number 4 (such as the four winds or four corners of the earth), what do you think is the significance of the apostles being divided into four groups of three?

POLISHING THE ART

The sculptures pictured on pages 14 and 15 show a remarkable change in the character of the twelve apostles. They went from the fear, conflict, and distraction Riemenschneider portrayed in the Last Supper to a focused group, centered on Jesus and even willing to die for him.

1 Read Matthew 28:16-20, a description of what happened after the resurrection of Jesus. Summarize these verses and tell why this short passage could be described as a turning point in the lives of the apostles.

Luke gives us more details about the time after the resurrection of Jesus and before the beginning of the church (Luke 24:36-53). Acts is a continuation of the book of Luke, telling how the church kept doing what "Jesus began to do and to teach" (Acts 1:1).

2 Read Acts 1:1-5. Underline all of the verbs in these verses that describe actions taken by Jesus after his resurrection. Over what period of time did this flurry of activity occur? From what you know of biblical history, do you think that number is significant? Why or why not?

A common view of Judaism of that day was that the Messiah (Christ) would come to throw off the oppression of the Roman government and physically rule as the king of a revived Jewish empire (see John 6:14, 15).

3 Notice the question asked by the apostles in Acts 1:6. What did they mean? How was their view of what Jesus wanted them to do much like that common view of their day?

4 Compare Jesus' words in Acts 1:7 to those he spoke before his crucifixion in Matthew 24:30-35. Why might the apostles have been a little disappointed to hear those words? How do they contrast with much modern teaching about the end of time?

5 Try to take the words of Matthew 28:18-20 and Acts 1:8 and combine them into one series of commands given by Jesus on that occasion. Note especially the word *authority* in Matthew 28:18 and the word *power* in Acts 1:8. How was this event a "transfer of power"? Why is that important?

Apparently, some in the early church thought the second coming was so near that they refused to fulfill their responsibilities of day-to-day life and simply waited for Jesus' return (see 2 Thessalonians 3:6-15).

6 Explain the importance of the following biblical commands for the church as we await the second coming of Jesus:

- Ephesians 5:15-17

- Hebrews 10:23-25

DISPLAYING THE MASTERPIECE

Review the activity that occurred between the time of Jesus' resurrection and the beginning of the church.

> The doubt of the apostles was alleviated through an intensive period of teaching, a demonstration of Jesus' power, and proof of his resurrection (Matthew 28:16-18; Acts 1:1-3).

> Jesus promised power to his disciples not just to survive but to thrive until the time he returns to earth (Matthew 28:20b; Acts 1:4, 5).

> The apostles were commanded to actively spread the gospel and to nurture one another until the time of Jesus' return (Matthew 28:19, 20; Acts 1:6-11).

1 How have you seen the church today . . .

help alleviate doubts of those who seek truth?

rely on the Holy Spirit rather than human strength alone?

go into all the world to preach the gospel?

2 Which of the following do you need the most as you wait for the end of time, and how might you go about getting it?

- "many convincing proofs" (Acts 1:3)

- "power from on high" (Luke 24:49)

- encouragement "toward love and good deeds" (Hebrews 10:24)

RESOURCES

BIBLE STUDY BOOKS

MacArthur, John F. *Twelve Ordinary Men* (Thomas Nelson, 2002).

McBirnie, William Steuart. *The Search for the Twelve Apostles* (Tyndale, 2008).

ART BOOKS

Sill, Gertrude Grace. *A Handbook of Symbols in Christian Art* (Touchstone, 1975).

Steffler, Alva William. *Symbols of the Christian Faith* (Eerdmans, 2002).

Stoddard, Whitney S. *Sculptors of the West Portals of Chartres Cathedral* (Norton, 1952).

WEB SITES

http://gallery.sjsu.edu/chartres/tour.html

http://www.biblegateway.com